A LOVE LETTER TO OURSELVES

AN ANTHOLOGY OF AFFIRMATIONS FROM AROUND THE WORLD

DR. CALENTHIA Y. MILLER

A 'Lure Publishing LLC

Copyright © 2024

A Love Letter to Ourselves: An Anthology of Affirmations from Around the World

By Dr. Calenthia Y. Miller

Library of Congress Control Number: 2024931291

ISBN: 979-8-9879903-9-1

First printing edition 2024

For information, contact:
www.alurepublishing.net
www.facebook.com/calenthiayvettemiller
www.alurepublishllc@gmail.com
www.facebook.com/alurepublishingllc
@calenthiamiller
@alurepublishing

www.canvasofthought.shop

DEDICATION

This book is a beautiful collaboration of inspiring individuals who have come together to emphasize the importance of self-perseverance and self-affirmation. Through their touching love letters, they showcase the uniqueness of their journeys, regardless of where they come from. The book is a testament to the power of self-love and serves as a beacon of hope for anyone seeking to overcome life's challenges.

Affirmation *noun*

af·fir·ma·tion

emotional support or encouragement

Table of Contents

REDISCOVERING WHO YOU ARE

INTRODUCTION

In these writings, each author has taken the opportunity to share their personal experiences and insights on the topic of affirmation. Their unique perspectives provide a more detailed and nuanced understanding of what affirmation means to them and how it has impacted their lives. By exploring the many facets of affirmation, the authors offer a rich tapestry of perspectives, each adding to our collective understanding of this vital concept.

Whether discussing the role of self-affirmation in building confidence or the power of external validation in fostering a sense of belonging, these writings provide a comprehensive and deeply personal exploration of affirmation and its impact on our lives.

What Does It Mean to Affirm Oneself?

Affirming oneself means recognizing and accepting our worthiness to receive love, care, support, and adoration. It involves understanding that we are deserving of these things simply because we exist and that settling for less is not an option. The words we speak to ourselves have immense value and can influence how we feel about ourselves and the world around us. Thus, committing to loving ourselves unconditionally is crucial, without limitations or self-imposed boundaries. Doing so can cultivate a positive and healthy relationship with ourselves, ultimately leading to a better quality of life.

It is also essential to mention love. It is crucial to integrate the concept of love and its role in self-affirmation and daily life. The notion of love holds significant importance in our lives, as it shapes our perception of ourselves and influences our interactions with others. Acknowledging how love impacts our daily routines, emotional well-being, and overall personal growth is essential. Therefore, incorporating this concept into our lives can lead to a more fulfilling and meaningful existence.

What is Love?

Love is a complex emotion that can take many forms, depending on the individuals involved. At its core, love is a deep and enduring feeling of affection and connection between two people. It is characterized by a sense of warmth, tenderness, and caring that is often difficult to put into words.

Love should be based on a foundation of trust, respect, and mutual understanding. It should be a safe space where both feel comfortable expressing their thoughts, feelings, and vulnerabilities without fear of judgment or rejection. Love should be unconditional, meaning that it is not contingent on the other person's behavior or actions.

In a healthy relationship, love should inspire personal growth and encourage both partners and individuals to be the best versions of themselves. It should be a source of motivation and inspiration rather than a cause of stress or anxiety. Love should be expressed through actions, not just words, and should be a priority.

DISCLAIMER: This book is a collection of love letters written by individuals who recognize the importance of self-perseverance and self-affirmation. These letters showcase the power of self-love and demonstrate that affirming oneself is crucial for personal growth and happiness, regardless of one's background. Through their heartfelt words, the writers inspire readers to embrace their unique stories and cherish the beauty of their journeys.

THE JOURNEY

THE JOURNEY

As we navigate through the unpredictable journey of life, we often encounter various obstacles and challenges that can be mentally and emotionally taxing. In these moments, it's important to remember the power of self-affirmation. This practice involves consciously acknowledging our positive attributes, accomplishments, and abilities and using them to boost our self-esteem and confidence.

Imagine having people willing to hold you accountable for your actions. These individuals are the ones who make sure that you live up to your potential, and they are always there to offer guidance and support when you need it the most. When you surround yourself with such people, you feel empowered to speak your name in their ears, knowing their lives will change for the better due to your interactions with them.

So, as you embark on your purpose this season, with each step you take, it's crucial to ensure that your actions align with your words. By doing so, you'll be able to make meaningful progress toward your goals while also inspiring those around you to do the same.

Seeking Understanding

The practice of self-affirmation is a powerful tool widely recognized for its positive impact on mental health and well-being. This practice involves focusing on our strengths, values, and accomplishments and acknowledging them in a way that reinforces our self-worth and boosts our confidence. Research shows that regular self-affirmation can help people cope with stress, anxiety, and other emotional challenges while promoting resilience and a more positive outlook on life.

Critical Things to Remember are:

- Get to know yourself.

- Be kind to yourself.

- Practice saying "no."

- Stop comparing yourself to others.

- Reward yourself just because.

- Find the good within yourself.

- Do what you love.

Affirmation is a universal concept that transcends cultural and societal boundaries and has been embraced by people from all walks of life. By incorporating self-affirmation into our daily routine, we can develop a more profound sense of self-awareness, appreciation, and acceptance. This, in turn, empowers us to face life's challenges with more confidence, optimism, and resilience.

Let's start our journey to understand the true meaning of self-affirmation from people worldwide, seen through their lens and written in their own words.

OUR LOVE LETTERS

CONQUER MY DEMONS

I ran away from home when I was 15 years old. I left an abusive relationship with my mother. I could not understand why she treated me so harshly. I was condemned regularly; nothing I did was good enough. I felt that life on the street would be better than living in a household that was destroying me. Thank goodness for my great-grandmother and grandmother; they gave me my redeeming qualities.

Although I stayed on the street until I was eighteen, I eventually moved in with my great-grandmother, who began my healing. For as long as I could remember, my emotional quotient has always been imbalanced with my ability to succeed in the physical realm of my life. I was unable to pursue my dreams because I was oblivious to how or what to do next, and all my attempts were followed by doubt, fear, and anger, which led to depression. I only pursued goals that would provide sustenance—nothing related to my true desires.

I tried to figure out and understand what and why I kept hitting that brick wall in pursuing my true dreams and heart yearnings. My great-grandma (Nana) was a true blessing. She encouraged me with love and understanding. I went back to school, received my GED, and then went on to college. During those days, my mother moved to another state, and because New York was getting bad, I eventually followed her because I had three children and wanted to get them into a new environment.

My Nana and grandmother told me, "You should go, but remember, your mother means you no good." I was not puzzled by those words; I knew what I had to do and proceeded to my destiny. I knew I had to break generational traumas—traumas that had become a generational curse. Fear, doubt, anger, and jealousy were the main components I had to remove and vanquish to heal. I realized that all these mechanisms were my hindrance. I grew up with them, so they were in my DNA, but now I had to change them.

First, recognizing what the problem was and coming to grips with it was tormenting because I had to release the ideology, teachings, and the person who initiated the trauma. I confronted my fears, doubts, anger, and jealousy, and for the first time in my life, I am free, and I am healing, one day at a time. The confidence squashed in my youth has returned vigorously at the age of sixty-nine. I learned that dream killers are not only people outside of your family circle, but they can also be people within. I recognized that my confidence in providing for myself and my family should also be applied to following my dreams, and I finally took that leap of faith.

LAVINA PRICE-WEAD

MY LOVE

It has been a while since you and I have spoken, and I must say I have missed you. Our time together has been a heck of a journey, and this has caused me to be reminiscent of the love we have. When was the last time I expressed that I am honored to be a part of your life? The thought of your very existence makes me smile. The woman that you have morphed into makes me even prouder. I recall the numerous times you expressed your concerns about your existence being a mistake. I can assure you, my love, that the essence of your existence is powerful in all dimensions.

You are such a resilient warrior. Do you know how I know? I was there with you through all your trials and tribulations, traumas, pains that you have embodied, losses you have suffered, and all of your deepest, darkest nights. Honestly, I could go on and on, but there is no need to because I already know that you see where I am going with that. You are an exemplary pillar of strength. Sis, when you walk into a room, the energy you emanate changes the climate. People stare at you in amazement and have no idea that you are who you are because of what you have been through. I am proud of you.

Despite everything you have been through, you're such a beautiful soul, inside and out. Your ignorance about life has caused you to make some not-so-wise decisions, but you accepted your consequences and kept moving forward. You go, girl! I have watched life knock you on your tail several times, but you bounced right back up as if you fell on a trampoline. I know, I know, I know. You are probably overthinking those very dark moments when you were ready to give up on life, but sis? You didn't! That is not the stock that you came from. Since I can remember you have memories, I know that you know you stand on the shoulders of your ancestors, and that makes you unstoppable!

You're such an inspiration, not only to your family but to people in your sphere of influence. When you come into someone's life, your essence causes them to elevate. You change the trajectory of people's lives. Sis, you are powerful. Your words move mountains, and the tone of your voice commands attention. Your younger generation looks up to you and although they have witnessed some of your unwise choices, that has not changed an iota of who you are to them. You are loving, caring, warm, firm, assertive, nonsensical, funny, understanding, talented, smart, intelligent, and wise, to name a few. You leave an imprint on the lives of those to whom you truly chose to give your love. You're dynamic and unforgettable!

I want to extend my sincerest apologies for taking so long to write you this letter. I know I have written many letters to you throughout the years; however, this is my first love letter. It definitely won't be my last, because I now know that you needed to read this. I love so many amazing things about you that I could write a few short stories. I know that you have a lot of situations in your life that demand your attention, so I will close this letter by letting you know that you will be hearing from me again sooner than you think. Allow me to leave you with this before I go: when you don't feel up to it or think you don't know what you should do, do it! You always figure it out along the way. I'll always be there for you. I love you, my love.

CLAUDETTE WHITE

HAVE I TOLD YOU I LOVE YOU?

Life is so short, I had to take a moment to put in writing that I love you. I remember when I didn't like you for being so easily distracted by your emotional decisions and how you allowed life to run amuck with no guidelines or guardrails. How you wished and hoped for your outcomes in life. Your arrogance was uncanny, yet you lacked the confidence to believe in yourself. The days of sitting and crying, the self-talk, self-evaluation, and self-correction are finally starting to pay off, I see.

Seeking help was your greatest milestone—staying on the course of healing and having the willingness to travel on that path to match the time you had lived in pain. A few weeks ago, when you finally spoke to your mother, I knew you were healed. I cheered for you. I screamed, "I love you." You are the person I have been seeking for decades. You were right under my nose, hidden in all of that mess.

Look at you today; you are stronger, kinder, greater, and at peace. You grew against all odds. Who would have known that "Kacky" was so lovable? Not only am I your greatest fan, I also openly tell everyone how much "I love you." Thank you for growing, not giving up on yourself, and being my greatest love affair.

PAUL A. POSEY

SHINE BRIGHT LIKE A DIAMOND

Hey beautiful,

It's been a while since I've reached out to you to connect with you, and for that, I apologize. I've been so overwhelmed with other people's issues—family matters, work obligations, and just making sure everyone else was taken care of—that I'd forgotten about you. Forgotten how important you are to me. Forgotten to show you how much I care about you. Forgotten to show you how much I love you. You deserve so much more time and attention than I have shown you. It's been far too long since I've shown you or even told you just how special and amazing you really are.

So much has happened in your life in the last few years. There's been a lot of loneliness and darkness weighing you down, but no one would know just by looking at you. You're still persevering and moving forward, all with a smile on your face. And that smile! It's beautiful and bright, like a diamond. But somewhere, I stopped noticing, appreciating your value, and giving you the proper care, and that diamond has become dull and listless.

I've neglected what made you shine. I neglected your relationship with God and didn't spend the time with Him that you needed to talk with him and allow him to lead and guide you. You had to fight unnecessarily for the peace that God so freely gives to his children. I am so sorry I put you through that. I neglected your need to be genuinely loved. Instead, I kept you in relationships with people who did everything to diminish your light. I allowed you to be with those who saw your value, who felt the high vibrations you radiate but only wanted to take your energy and did nothing to pour it back into you. I allowed others to use you until there was nothing left, and for that, I am truly sorry.

You deserve so much more than what I have given you for far too long. You had a spark. Correction...You HAVE A FIRE within you that radiates energy that changes the atmosphere of any room you walk into. People take notice. Your vibe is almost intoxicating. I promise I will no longer neglect you. I will nurture you. I will give you everything you need that's within my power. You will be, and you ARE the most important person in my life, and no one will ever come before you again. You are absolutely amazing, and I love you with every fiber of my being today, tomorrow, and forever more.

CHIKETTA S. LANE

RENEWED LOVE

Girl, look at you! What's that saying? "I'm so glad I don't look like what I've been through!" All praise, glory, and honor go to my Heavenly Father for sustaining me and constantly showing me mercy, grace, favor, and unconditional love.

Every day, as I look into the mirror of my mind, I reflect on my life. I think about the hurt, pain, anger, rage, and disappointments I've experienced. I'd been holding on to these emotions for a long time because I believed they protected me from getting hurt again. I've been in attack mode for so long that I find allowing love, peace, patience, or forgiveness challenging. I've struggled with finding my self-worth, which I lost over the years. Encouraging myself every day feels like I'm working another job. I'm not a fake person, but sometimes the sadness and loneliness lurking deep within me overshadow my laughter, smiles, upbeat attitude, and ability to bring joy to the room. Even though I'm often told I'm the sunshine in the room, I'm always bottling up my screams because I can't let anyone see how I truly feel.

Who am I? Throughout my life, I have always tried to please those around me. However, at fifty-six years old, I still feel lost. Giving up is not an option for me, as it is not in my nature. Father God, you have helped me through many challenging and painful times. You have taught me to love myself again, let go of past hurts, heal, forgive, and live my life! You have restored my soul! Although it has been a slow process, when I look in the mirror now, I can smile and say, "I am uniquely made like no other. My Father assigned me a purpose, and I am a child of God." Lisa, always remember that when God comes first in your life, there is only victory, triumph, joy, peace, and love! Keep following where God is leading and guiding you. Stay steadfast, encouraged, and grounded in your faith and beliefs, knowing He is always by your side.

Love you, girl!

LISA FIELDS

A LOVE LETTER TO MYSELF

Be strong and of good courage; the Lord is with you, and He will never forsake you. You are fearfully and wonderfully made by the magnificent Creator himself, and he makes no mistakes.

You are strong, confident, and intelligent. You are who God made you to be. Even though you second-guess yourself a lot and feel unworthy, know that God loves you and you are His child!

I love your giving spirit. I love how you care for others so unselfishly. Your generosity does not go unnoticed.

You wear your heart on your sleeve, which can sometimes take you to a place where darkness lies. Your tenacity keeps you from falling into that abyss and struggling to stay close to the Light. The Light is where your strength is.

This letter is meant to encourage you. You are more than what you see; you are loved and cared for, and even though you may not see it, you are needed, and without you, others would suffer. YOU MATTER! Never forget that. I love you, and you should love yourself too!

Sincerely,

ANDREA BEALE

REFLECTIONS OF A HEARTFELT JOURNEY OF LEARNING TO LOVE THY SELF

Dearest Self,

In the quiet spaces of my heart, I want you to know that I love you, even though I may not always show it. Your courage to embrace life in all its facets, to venture into the unknown unafraid of failure, has created the riches of experiences that life has bestowed upon you. If it were not for you being open to trying new things, you would not have become who you are today, from completing projects to being a publisher and everything in between. Just know that you are still becoming.

I love you for daring to defy conventions, accepting your imperfections, and forging your own blueprint. I am grateful for your role as a follower, recognizing that it's the very essence that allows you to lead. The unbelievable thing is that people will follow you because they believe in you.

Your audacity to create, develop, and be your authentic self, letting your heart lead you to become your own beacon of inspiration, is amazing. You have navigated through the diverse roles of life, and you don't always do it with grace. My only prayer is that you begin to take your health seriously and shower love on your family and friends because they are your pillars of strength; you need them. No one can survive in this world alone.

So, as you go into each new day, learn to love hard and build trust despite its challenges, because there is nothing like it. You will have stories to tell your children and grandchildren. Through the 3-ring circus, the engagement ring, the wedding ring, and the suffer-ring, you continue to keep him coming home with love for now. Things can change in a split second.

Remember, everything you desire is attainable because you are His child. You are a cherished child by your father and mother, embraced by a divine love that knows no bounds. Remember what Terry said, "Every day we are dying," so why not move mountains? You're an ordinary person who dreams of doing extraordinary things, so why not do it now? Continue to put out in the atmosphere what you desire and watch as it comes to life. Don't be afraid to call the banker for that building you desire. Don't be afraid. If not now, then when?

People are counting on you, so as you navigate the twists and turns, seize the reins of life with confidence, getting plenty of rest and water because it's not just about you; it's about all of His children, even the ones in your possession.

With boundless love,

SHENITHA FINESSE ANNIECE

GOD, FAMILY, AND LOVE-SOUL AFFIRMATION

Do you ever feel like you don't have control over your own life, and it just spirals out of control and leads you down a road that you didn't intend to take, even when some of it is familiar or caused by your own choices or trauma?

This letter was written to encourage you that no matter what you go through in life, you can still be successful. I used my pain as an opportunity to gain empowerment to fulfill my purpose by using the gift of compassion and love that God gave me for the people. I grew up in the church with a two-parent home and was always taught right from wrong, but that didn't stop me from getting slammed with adversity. I had to find my own faith in God while learning to handle every punch life threw at me.

I had to learn that being a good man was not enough, and I had to be a great guy to create the lifestyle I deserved for my family and me. I have gone through a divorce, failed time after time, was discredited as a father, made mistakes, had to comfort others when I did not know how to comfort myself, had doors slammed in my face, lost a child, experienced grief, experienced financial struggles, been emotionally and physically injured, and even been hated and overlooked.

The key is that I never gave up and eventually had to find courage and confidence in myself. Despite all that, I had to dig deep and elevate myself to greatness. So, using my pain as motivation to get to the next level, I changed my mindset and learned to control my emotions, remain disciplined, work hard in silence, and start believing I was exceptional.

Today, I am the proud father of five amazing children, husband to a beautiful and loving wife, a military veteran, a master's degree holder, a career man, and on a journey to create an empire as a business owner, life coach, and entrepreneur. This love letter is a testament to what true dedication can create for a man who could have given up a long time ago. If I can do it, you can get your life back on track and accomplish whatever you want. The road or path you think you will take is not always the one God will lead you to. If you keep God first and family second and love yourself, he will never fail you. So, find your reason to live, love, and trust God in the midst of it all.

You got this!

BERNARD DYSON, JR

THIS IS MY LOVE LETTER TO YOU!

My journey to self-love started after a therapy session.

I had stopped looking in the mirror for years; I would brush my teeth and look at only my mouth. I would wash my face and not look at my reflection; sometimes, I would put on makeup and not make eye contact. I stopped caring what I looked like; I stopped talking to people who truly were for me; I wanted to sleep all the time. It took until I was forty to blossom into the rose I am today.

I was depressed and did not know it, and I had been depressed for over fifteen years. I was in a deep sleep, and when I woke up, I was forty pounds heavier. I had lost teeth and hair, a few calls, and some friends along the way. I am now on the road to recovery and acceptance.

There are a few things I had to learn.

Self-love has to be done on purpose and unapologetically; love yourself from your toenails to your hair follicles, and love yourself deep into your soul.

I learned that self-love is the very first romance.

So, how can you love someone else if you cannot love yourself?

Love is not a quick fad or a one-hit wonder; when someone genuinely loves you, they will always love you through the good and bad and times when you feel lost and broken.

This you must do for yourself: love yourself through every challenge.

I had to love and forgive myself for all the times I did not know how to love or didn't understand it. I allowed myself to be misused and mistreated by others because I felt like I deserved it.

Once I realized I was my only advocate, love was sweet and understanding, and patience awaited me.

I have learned that there are levels to self-love; to get there, you must vibrate higher by starting a spiritual journey. Eat right and be the best version of yourself possible. Surround yourself with people who love and pour affirmations into you; accept yourself for everything you are and are not; and welcome all the possibilities in between.

This was my journey to self-love, and everyone's journey will differ. But the first step in learning self-love is understanding the true meaning of LOVE and yourself.

ELOGEIA HADLEY

FINALLY SEEN

Beautiful, dark-skinned, nappy-headed child who grew from a little girl to a young woman who was always busy doing good deeds for others yet still felt invisible. If only I could let you know... I see you.

You've taken care of the elderly with love your entire life without even questioning whether you feel like doing it. You've housed people experiencing homelessness because a house is a structure, but a home is where they are loved by that huge heart of yours.

You're even trying to end the strife within the family because you know that "Blessed are the peacemakers, for they shall be called the children of God." I love that you're truly grateful to God for your strength and health. You've walked and jogged more miles than most people drive in their cars.

You work tirelessly, filling your days maintaining your own landscaping and being your brother's keeper by working on your neighbor's lawn, too. You were tired of trying to run your own life, so you gave your life to God by accepting the Lord Jesus as your savior so you could live in peace for eternity with the Father—no tears, no pain, no struggle. Why would we bother if we didn't have all that to look forward to?

    I love how strong every trial and tribulation has made you. You're the courageous woman of God that we all see. You've sacrificed, worked, and fought hard for everything when life was tough, but you never gave up. Thank you for honoring GOD by being selfless, kind, honest, joyful, peaceful, and living every day by grace through faith and hope.

GAYNELLE JACKSON-BURNSIDE

A LOVE LETTER TO THE YOUNGER ME

As you go through life, you will run into challenges. You won't feel like you will make it through some of them. I need you to know that you are stronger than you think. Trust your father and grandmother; they will protect you from many things. When you feel the need to drink, know there's a solution; hold on. Remember that as you walk this path set for you, you are stronger than you think; never give up and keep pushing. I promise you that what seems like the end of the world will get better.

Looking in the mirror today, I never thought I would have survived the drinking and the mental abuse. I had to bury four people in a span of six years. I know it was by the grace of God that I made it. Doubt was creeping in for many days, and the obstacles I faced seemed insurmountable. I didn't think I could walk ahead, knowing every struggle was a test. You can't have a testimony without a test. Every setback was a chapter to be written in this book of my life. Every challenge that I met and conquered was a life lesson.

Everything that I thought was going against me was going for me. It took until I was in my fifties to see that the world was not against me. It laid the foundation for me to grow into the best version of myself.

Looking in the mirror, I am blessed that I had my father and grandmother to help me get through the rough times when I didn't think I would make it. I am proud of the person I have become.

Thank you, younger me, for never giving up on yourself. Thank you for leaning on your father and grandmother. Thank you for getting us to where we are today.

PAMELA JAMES COLEMAN

FINDING MY WAY

Looking back on my life, I realize just how blessed I am. My mother raised me; my father was present sometimes and contributed financially but did not spend much time with me. My mother didn't spend much quality time with me either, because she worked all day doing her best to raise and support seven children. Thinking back on my upbringing, with so many siblings under one roof, I no longer wonder why I had to learn to love myself early in life. I am not saying that my mother and father did not love me.

My mother did not have time to give me much individual attention, and my father was not around much because he lived in another state for most of my childhood. I was shy and had low self-esteem as a young child. One of my older siblings helped me realize my full potential and encouraged me into adulthood. She was a great example of what it means to love yourself and others. I wasn't always confident in what I did or attempted to do, but the extra encouragement certainly gave me a sense of who I was. I learned to believe in myself and find my way in life.

After giving birth in my senior year of high school and struggling as a young mother yet determined to finish high school, with the encouragement of my family, I was certain that pursuing my education beyond high school was not an option. I never lost focus on where my awesome God had brought me from and where he was trying to lead me.

As a child and now an independent adult, I am elated that my siblings were and continue to be perfect examples of showing love to each other and helping others. I did not always love myself, but with God's guidance, loving myself became a permanent fixture of my character. Loving others and sharing my blessings come easily from within.

I am retired after thirty-three years in education and returned ten additional years as an educator. I am thrilled that I will leave the work sector in a few months to enjoy some quality time. Loving yourself first makes one's steps in life so much easier!

DANZIOLA JOHNSON

REFLECTIONS

As I reflect on my life, I think about the challenges and successes I have encountered throughout my journey. My story is not complicated, but it is "my story," and I am content with the choices I have made over the years. There were several obstacles and distractions in life, but there was always a lesson to be learned from every situation. I have always identified myself as an independent woman in charge of my destiny—a career-driven, self-motivating, strong force to be reckoned with.

As I sashay into my fifties, I have discovered that it's okay to be vulnerable, allowing others inside my circle while simultaneously maintaining the role of being my biggest advocate. During a coaching session, I was asked, "What are your hobbies?" I paused momentarily and said, "Can you repeat the question?" My coach asked again, "What do you enjoy doing when you're not at work?" I was speechless. I did not have a hobby, and I didn't indulge in anything that pleased my heart other than work.

It was at that moment that I decided to take charge of my personal life. I am learning to take mental health days if only to relax and do absolutely "nothing." I pledge to myself to take more time enjoying life, myself, and my family today, as tomorrow is not promised.

PATRICE L. BONDO

THINGS I'LL NEVER FORGET

In life, we are presented with a constant revolving door called "the inevitable." These are the things we can't predict or control and wish we could live without. Well, that would be the case for most people. But for me, I'm a fan of obstacles and inconvenience. I feel as though the challenges we face determine who we will be and how we will get there. Who are you when your back is against the wall?

In times of hardship, I am reminded of my character, morals, and will for greatness. The ability to stand tall when the weight of the world is on your shoulders, pushing you with blunt force towards the ground, is a reflection of who you determined you would be. Since I was a little boy, I have decided that my life has more purpose than just serving myself; my power has always been my ability to remain positive and understand that my smile, calm, and strength fuel the light of so many others.

When faced with challenges that would be detrimental to most, I remain solidified in who I truly am. Oftentimes, I am asked the simple question, "How?" The answer is simple. I learned to love myself so much that my love for others became my fuel in return. When in doubt of my powers, I look in the mirror and face the only person that matters to me. Looking yourself in the eyes and having honest conversations within is the only way you'll ever be able to have an external conversation of any relevance.

The love others place on you will only bounce right off if you don't have that love for yourself internally. I know that I am impactful, I know that I am rich in blessings, and I know that my journey has been ordained to be purposeful. Each day, I wake up and understand the power of my tongue. So, I tell myself that I am worthy of a day of positivity; I tell myself that my day will be productive yet peaceful; and, most importantly, I tell myself that I love myself.

For generations, we have created curses that have haunted us mentally by simply ignoring the importance of the truth. The truth is that life is hard! So hard that it will make you curl up in a ball and throw in the towel. The old me threw in that towel before, and the Most High threw it right back. I wish the old me loved me; I wish the old me knew my strength; and I wish the old me didn't have to suffer so much. I am a king and destined for a throne of higher purpose. So, I write this letter to myself as a reminder of the times when I felt I wasn't deserving. I am deserving! Dear me, make sure you always love yourself.

ANDRE SANSBURY JR

GRIND, GRIT, GRACE

Hey, pretty lady!

Yeah, You! Or would you rather I say, "Hey gurl, Heeeyyy!" in my strong southern accent?

Either way, I need a moment of your time.

I need you to go get a mirror because, after you finish reading this letter, I want you to look at yourself! Really, LOOK at yourself!

It's not going to be easy to accept, but I need you to take heed.

First, I hate to tell you that everyone doesn't like you, everyone ain't going to be nice to you, and people really don't think about you as often as you think they do.

I'm sorry that it has taken me forty-seven years, four kids, and a husband to write this letter.

But let's be real; up to this point, you have just been watering bad seeds.

Don't get me wrong, I'm not saying that your life has been meaningless; I'm saying you're investing too much of yourself and not seeing a return.

I love you enough to say, "STOP wasting your time on people and things that don't add value to your existence."

Now FOCUS!

Focus on YOU! Be selfish!

That relationship (with a significant other, job, or friend) that you have all that "history" with is over.

Accept it.

Grieve it.

S***, you can even talk about it.

But I don't have any expectations!

Let it be like vomit.

Spit that s*** out and move the f**** on!

FOCUS!

You are too good for those who have walked away from you! Don't take s*** personally. Let it be. I love you enough to tell you three words that should map out your days. They may not make life easier, but when you are focused on one thing, other things are usually blurred.

FOCUS! I want you to focus on three words EVERY DAY: grind, grit, and grace.

Your grind will give you purpose! Wake up every day with an objective! Decide to accomplish something so that you don't waste any time that has been loaned to you.

Your grit will be your fuel. Push through your day and pull away from uncomfortable situations. Be cautious of how much you allow yourself to be pushed and pulled, so you don't risk losing your wits.

Your grace will be your happy place. It will provide a barrier between you and the world you can't control. Hold your head high as you make deliberate eye contact. Don't apologize for being you! Walk into every room like you belong there. Speak with conviction so that people know you are not to be played with.

Now, put on some red lipstick, buy yourself a good bra and a cheap bottle of wine, pick up that mirror, and call it a day!

RAQUEL WELLS-WILLIAMS

UNLOCKING THE INSPIRATION FROM WITHIN

You've come from the roughest terrain,

Only to land on the greenest grass.

Life comes at us fast;

We don't know how long it's destined to last.

I think about a boy born from parents

Who originated in the Caribbean Sea.

A land once known as the island of Pearl

Has since disintegrated into poverty.

The exquisite island frequently dined
On cornmeal, rice, sauce, and kola champagne.

Once a blissful, carefree life,

embalmed by sea and palm trees,

now gripped in pain.

Shackled by government economies

And gripped by gang crimes and starvation.

The time had arrived for the beleaguered citizens

To flee the once proud nation.

But it turned out that the fleeing parents

Would trade one prison for another.

Imprisoned by a language barrier in a strange land

Separated from brother and sister.

Palm trees give way to skyscrapers

As jungles of leaves become buildings of steel.

Working endlessly in a city that never sleeps

A reality once thought of as surreal.

But an endless movie reel would best describe

the immigrants' mundane existence,

Compelled to repeat an endless routine

to work down to the bone with no resistance.

They would birth a young king

Whose mind was saturated with wonder and intrigue,

Despite his peers telling him

That he was insignificant and out of their league.

His surroundings and circumstances

constantly served as a reminder of his limitations.

Society strived to censor his thoughts,

but he found his spiritual salvation.

An initiation in the form of literary,

artistic, and lyrical verbs of self-expression.

Learning that his power was within his body, soul, and mind,

freeing his creativity,

While adapting to this newfound gift

that he once concealed with exclusivity.

A community burst forth from the King's cerebral cortex,

leaving his doubters vexed.

The doors of inspiration burst open,

and all ideas were forged, both simple and complex.

Unleash the intricate mindset

that has been longing to be unlocked and released.
The more you cultivate your subconscious,

the more inspiration will never cease.

MARC "BLACK CYRANO" BEAUSEJOUR

SHINE YOUR LIGHT

My dear child,

You did not have the best of beginnings! You were found abandoned on a roadside in Uganda as a two- or three-day-old baby.

You were adopted at a time when illegitimacy was frowned upon by the community, and when it was discovered you were not Asian but of dual heritage, that led to you being shunned even more. You were Asian-African, and mixed relationships were taboo at that time, the offspring of those liaisons even more so.

Your Asian adoptive parents did their best to shield you from the hurtful comments from the community, but you could not be totally protected. The darkness of prejudicial attitudes still seeped through. Racism, Colorism, and Sexism were the cloaks that enveloped your being day and night. It was hard to shake off the mantle of self-hate they induced in you.

I am so happy to see you now, my Ray of Light. You have finally shaken off that negativity with the help of the Divine and the guidance and support of the legion of angels. The angels and I say this to you: "Be yourself. Speak your truth always, and be confident that you are enough. Do not depend on anyone's likes or dislikes of you as a person. Remember, you are worthy and came into this life with a purpose: to shine your light and radiate your message of acceptance of yourself and others to the world.

Look in the mirror and believe it when you say, I am beautiful on the outside and within. I measure my beauty through being kind to others and animals. My beauty helps me appreciate all that Mother Earth has provided and respect my environment and surroundings. My beauty lies within my humanity and abhorrence for hatred and bigotry in all its forms. My beauty is not measured by my skin color, the texture of my hair, or my size.

Don't rely on the shallow and transient standards of what society calls beautiful. Shine your light and walk tall, my beautiful African-Asian Queen."

BHARTI DHIR

UNMASKING WHO I AM

Hello, gorgeous,

Reflecting on my life, I realize I have spent most of it living a life that wasn't mine. I felt like an imposter, pretending to be someone I wasn't and living my life according to what others expected of me. For too long, I couldn't hear my voice, drowned out by the voices of others who told me who I was and what I should do. Their words constantly reminded me of my flaws and shortcomings, making me feel inadequate and unworthy.

I spent most of my days seeking approval and validation from others, always looking for someone to tell me I was good enough. I didn't realize that the love and validation I sought had to come from within me. I was lost, searching for something I couldn't find, unaware that the answers I sought were already inside me.

My liberation came when I stopped expecting people to fulfill an expectation they could not. I learned that people have limitations and can't always meet our expectations. I stopped seeking validation from others and started looking for it within myself. I realized that the only person who could genuinely validate and love me was me.

Courage is built during the storms we have weathered. I permit myself to walk in my purpose and never allow my naysayers to devalue who I am and the path I am traveling. I know self-doubt is like a weed that can grow and take over if you don't uproot it.

I affirm daily that loving myself is the most important thing I can do for myself. My greatness is like a rare gem that only a select few are worthy of seeing. I know my existence is everything, even though those around me may have counted me out. I am determined to live on my terms, being true to myself, living the life I was meant to live, and living and loving myself without boundaries.

DR CALENTHIA Y. MILLER

REDISCOVERING WHO YOU ARE

REDISCOVERING WHO YOU ARE

As you continue on this journey of self-discovery, you must conduct self-checks and inventory. It is crucial to allow yourself grace when you can't tolerate unnecessary chaos and confusion. This might mean you must reconsider those who no longer serve a purpose in this season of your life. It doesn't mean you don't care for them. It simply means that you have outgrown each other. This happens in so many relationships. Self-preservation is critical to survival.

Survival Guide to Self-Preservation

- Set boundaries.

- Prioritize free time versus available time.

- Allocate downtime to relax and regroup.

- Nourish your mind, body, and spirit.

- Love yourself.

- Again, set boundaries. Cut off anything that may harm you.

Although change can be a daunting experience, it is essential to acknowledge its significance and welcome it with open arms.

Remaining static and unchanging can lead to a lack of growth and progress. Start practicing the act of self-love; it will give you unspeakable joy.

In addition, sharing your experiences can be a powerful tool for personal growth, connecting with others, and creating positive change. Whether it's a triumph or a difficult challenge you've overcome, your story can inspire and motivate those around you. It can also help you process and reflect on your experiences, gaining new insights and perspectives. So, never underestimate the value of your experiences, and don't be afraid to share them with others. Your story may be precisely what someone else needs to hear.

You Have the Power. It's in You.

Investing in yourself is the greatest gift you can give yourself. Every day when you wake up, take a moment to reflect on the unique gifts that the universe has bestowed upon you. Whether it's your intelligence, creativity, or compassion, acknowledge and appreciate these qualities. Remember that you have the power to make your dreams a reality and that by nurturing your potential, you can achieve greatness.

A positive self-image is a foundation for greater confidence and developing a higher sense of self-worth. I also suggest working with a good, licensed therapist. A therapist is your advocate and provides a safe, judgment-free environment. It's okay not to be okay.

Continue to affirm who you are daily through simple affirmations or inspirational quotes.

Instruction

Read the affirmation or inspirational quote entirely. It is okay if you must reread it a second time for clarity. Once you have read, take some time to dissect and reflect on the words, and think of a situation or event that may be relevant.

Now, it is time to respond. Remember, no answer is the wrong answer. It is what you think.

Read

"I will never be the obstacle that prevents me from reaching my goal."

_____

_____

_____

_____

Reflect

_____

_____

_____

_____

Response

_____

_____

_____

_____

_____

_____

Read

"I am beautiful, bold, and inherently great beyond measure."

_____

_____

_____

_____

_____

_____

Reflect

_____

_____

_____

_____

_____

Response

_____

_____

_____

_____

_____

_____

Read

"I am more than what the naked eye can see."

_____

_____

_____

_____

_____

Reflect

_____

_____

_____

_____

_____

Response

_____

_____

_____

_____

_____

Read

"I am intentionally investing in the best version of me."

_____

_____

_____

_____

_____

Reflect

_____

_____

_____

_____

Response

_____

_____

_____

_____

_____

Read

"I am in control of the direction in which I am traveling."

_____

_____

_____

_____

_____

Reflect

_____

_____

_____

_____

Response

_____

_____

_____

_____

_____

Read

"I refuse to operate in situations that consist of chaos, confusion or drama."

_____

_____

_____

_____

_____

_____

Reflect

_____

_____

_____

_____

_____

Response

_____

_____

_____

_____

_____

Create Your Own Words of Affirmations or Inspiration

Write

_____

_____

_____

_____

_____

_____

Reflect

_____

_____

_____

_____

_____

Response

_____

_____

_____

_____

_____

Write

_____
_____
_____
_____
_____
_____

Reflect

_____
_____
_____
_____
_____

Response

_____
_____
_____
_____
_____

Write

_____

_____

_____

_____

_____

Reflect

_____

_____

_____

_____

Response

_____

_____

_____

_____

_____

Write

Reflect

Response

Write

_____

_____

_____

_____

_____

Reflect

_____

_____

_____

_____

_____

Response

_____

_____

_____

_____

_____

Write

_____

_____

_____

_____

_____

_____

Reflect

_____

_____

_____

_____

_____

Response

_____

_____

_____

_____

_____

Write

_____

_____

_____

_____

_____

_____

Reflect

_____

_____

_____

_____

_____

Response

_____

_____

_____

_____

_____

_____

Write

_____

_____

_____

_____

_____

_____

Reflect

_____

_____

_____

_____

_____

Response

_____

_____

_____

_____

_____

Write

Reflect

Response

"LOVE YOURSELF BEYOND THE BOUNDARIES."

"YOUR FREEDOM IS IN YOUR HANDS"

Your Love Letter

_____

_____

_____

_____

_____

_____

_____

_____

_____

_____

_____

_____

_____

_____

_____

_____

_____

_____

_____

_____

_____

_____

_____

Your Love Letter

Your Love Letter

Your Love Letter

"EMBRACE YOU!"

"NO TIME TO BE STAGNANT"

SPECIAL THANKS TO OUR CO-AUTHORS

LAVINA PRICE-WEAD

CLAUDETTE WHITE

PAUL A. POSEY

CHIKETTA S. LANE

LISA FIELDS

ANDREA BEALE

BERNARD DYSON JR

SHENITHA FINESSE ANNIECE

ELOGEIA HADLEY

GAYNELLE JACKSON-BURNSIDE

PAMELA JAMES COLEMAN

DANZIOLA JOHNSON

PATRICE L. BONDO

ANDRE SANSBURY JR

RAQUEL WELLS-WILLIAMS

MARC "BLACK CYRANO" BEAUSEJOUR

BHARTI DHIR

DR. CALENTHIIA Y. MILLER

WORDS OF WISDOM

As you continue your journey, remember to take time to appreciate the unique beauty within you. Remember, you are made up of many qualities, traits, and experiences that make you who you are. Embrace your strengths and acknowledge your weaknesses, for they are all part of what makes you unique. Take pride in your accomplishments, and keep pushing yourself to grow and learn. Always remember that you are a beautiful and valuable human being and that your presence in this world is essential.

Dr. Calenthia Y. Miller

"YOU ARE WORTH IT, AND YOUR

EXISTENCE IS GREATLY NEEDED."

"LOVING ME IS NOT UP FOR DISCUSSION."

"MOMENTS OF INCONSISTENCY ARE MINUTES OF WASTED TIME."

COMING SOON

A LOVE LETTER: THE WORLD OWES ME NOTHING!